ANTHONY
BURGESS

CHILDHOOD

D0588193

PENGUIN BOOKS

PENGUIN BOOKS

Published by the Penguin Group. Penguin Books Ltd, 27 Wrights Lane, London
w8 5tz, England. Penguin Books USA Inc., 375 Hudson Street, New York,
New York 10014, USA. Penguin Books Australia Ltd, Ringwood, Victoria, Australia.
Penguin Books Canada Ltd, 10 Alcorn Avenue, Toronto, Ontario, Canada m4v 3b2.
Penguin Books (NZ) Ltd, 182–190 Wairau Road, Auckland 10, New Zealand · Penguin
Books Ltd, Registered Offices: Harmondsworth, Middlesex, England · This
extract is from *Little Wilson and Big God* by Anthony Burgess, first published by
William Heinemann Ltd 1987. Published in Penguin Books 1988. This edition pub-
lished 1996. Copyright © Anthony Burgess, 1987. All rights reserved · Typeset by
Rowland Phototypesetting Ltd, Bury St Edmunds, Suffolk. Printed in England by
Clays Ltd, St Ives plc ·
Except in the United States of America, this book is sold
subject to the condition that it shall not, by way of trade or otherwise, be lent,
re-sold, hired out, or otherwise circulated without the publisher's prior consent
in any form of binding or cover other than that in which it is published and without a similar condition including this condition being imposed on the subsequent
purchaser · 10 9 8 7 6 5 4 3 2 1

Wedged as we are between two eternities of idleness, there is no excuse for being idle now . . .

I was born when the war was at its grimmest, on February 25, 1917. Unrestricted submarine warfare had begun at the beginning of the month, though food rationing was not to come in until my first birthday. England was still stunned by the death of a finger-pointing icon: Lord Kitchener had been drowned on June 5, 1916, when the *Hampshire* struck a mine. The battle of the Somme, which had begun a month later, had whimpered to an end on November 13, with 420,000 British losses – a figure as hard to visualize as great wealth. But the Americans declared war on April 6, 1917, and on June 26 their first contingents arrived in France. I was not quite a month old when the Leningraders rehearsed the October Revolution. My birth thus coincided with that of the modern age – American world hegemony, the dissolution of Christendom. I yelled my Otto Rank anger at the light just as the Sunday pubs were opening. A child of the Fishes, I was thirsty as a fish: the lactal ducts could never refill fast enough.

February 25 is the feast day of saints and martyrs not much regarded – Victorinus and his companions, Caesarius of Nazianzus, the virgin Walburga, the bishops Tarasius and Gerland, Ethelbert of Kent. In 1601 it was an Ash Wednesday and the day of the execution of the Earl of Essex – one of those historical dates I can never forget. It is the birthday of musicians – Caruso, Myra Hess, of the impressionist painter Pierre Renoir, above all of the dramatist Carlo Goldoni, with whom I have always felt a faint affinity. The day before is the birthday of George Moore and of Arnold Dolmetsch, the day before that of George Frederick Handel. The day after honours Victor Hugo, Honoré Daumier, and Buffalo Bill. How much truth there is in astrology I do not know, but the first fortnight of Pisces certainly presides over arts to which I was attracted about equally in my youth. I spent too long deciding which art to follow – music, writing, drawing, the popular stage. It was not until I was thirty-seven that I became a writer. Certainly I had to be an artist of some kind or other. My father breathed beer on me and said: 'He may be a new Napoleon.' Not Wellington. The Catholic North-West, like Ireland, had looked to the French being on the sea, and the decay of the Orange.

One's first memories are often vicarious: one is told that one did something or was involved in something; one dramatizes it and folds the image falsely into the annals of the truly remembered. So, less than two years old, I am sitting on a shoulder in Manchester's Piccadilly while a flag-waving crowd cheers the Armistice. Then the lights go out. In early

1919 my father, not yet demobilized, came on one of his regular, probably irregular, furloughs to Carisbrook Street to find both my mother and sister dead. The Spanish influenza pandemic had struck Harpurhey. There was no doubt of the existence of a God: only the supreme being could contrive so brilliant an afterpiece to four years of unprecedented suffering and devastation. I, apparently, was chuckling in my cot while my mother and sister lay dead on a bed in the same room. I should not have been chuckling; I should have been howling for food; perhaps the visiting neighbour who had herself just been stricken had provided me with a bottle of Glaxo. My father's attitude to his son must now have become too complicated for articulation. It would have been neater if all three in that room had been obliterated. When I was old enough to appreciate his mingled resentment and factitious gratitude at my survival, I was able to understand his qualified affection, his lack of interest in any future I might have, the ill-considered second marriage which was a way of getting me off his hands.

Of my sister Muriel he passed on no memories. My mother survived briefly in vague reminiscences of the Manchester music hall – a voice that could ride over a restive audience, the shining abundant hair, the neat ankles. When she herself became part of an audience she was a comedian's gift: her laugh was loud and primed general laughter. As a housewife she had no further duty to the lissom shape that had been her professional pride. She took to Guinness and

3

boiled puddings. It would be easier to recreate her in fiction, relating her to Molly Bloom and Rosie Driffield, than to wrestle with a virtually non-existent reality. It is difficult to know how far we have an obligation to the dead. I sometimes resent my father's failure to introduce me even to her insubstantial after-image, but he spoke little of her. She joined the great boneyard of the war and its aftermath. My father went back to Swift's Beef Market, bought a straw hat, took heavily to draught Bass, and waited for the cleansing 1920s.

I come to full consciousness in a terraced house on Delauneys Road, Higher Crumpsall, in the care of my mother's sister, Ann Bromley. She was a war widow with two daughters, Elsie and Betty. Opposite the house was a great infirmary where, I learned, people were cut open. This gratuitous slashing and slitting seemed reasonable to me, who must have absorbed by osmosis the ethos of the times. My father was a lodger, visible mainly on Friday evenings, when he brought home a prime joint from the beef market. For the rest of the time he drank or tried to cut down on his drinking by playing the piano in one of the local cinemas. He then combined both diversions by becoming the regular pianist at the Golden Eagle, a huge pub on Lodge Street, Miles Platting. There he met his second wife, who was the widowed landlady. In 1922 I was told that she was my new mother. Before then I called my aunt mother.

There is no magic in the word: it is the name a child will happily give to any woman who looks after him. It did not follow that Elsie and Betty were my sisters. I hear myself calling at the age of three and a half, with a Lancashire vowel: 'Mother, mother – there's a donkey on the road.' A workman had knocked on the door asking for hot water for his tea can. He said: 'You're a big baby, shouting for your mother because you see a donkey.' I did not know what he meant – fear of the donkey, wonder at it? How, anyway, did I know it was a donkey? Across the road, behind that gaunt façade of many windows, the cutting up of living bodies was calmly proceeding.

I slept alone in a cold room with one picture on the wall. It was of a gipsy woman looking balefully and pointing a finger. I was told that the legend beneath it was 'Beware'. When I thought I was asleep the picture would open on loud hinges and disclose the world of cutting up live but uncomplaining bodies. It was lighted by fire. I was given the choice of joining the bodies or else remaining where I was, in the big lumpy flock bed which was steadily filling with horse shit and turning into Delauneys Road. The turds were turning into aromatic serpents with teeth. I would scream and scream, and my aunt would come in her night-dress to see what the trouble was. The trouble was the picture, but it was not removed. I was never taken into her bed. After so much public horror, what was a mere child's nightmare?

The house was damp and looked out on a damp back garden which was full of slugs and, I feared, snakes. I was

5

shown a picture of Christ being laid in his tomb. I asked what was happening. A male voice said: 'They're going on a journey.' It must have been the voice of a local boy named Stevie, who sometimes had dinner with us. Among the peas on his plate was a black one. He impaled it on his fork and said: 'My name is Stevie Blackpea.' Blackpea had to be some relation of Blackpool, where I must sometime have been taken. I can remember only a railway compartment with a black pool outside it: etymology was drawing me slowly to a life of words. I had new dreams in which Christ was laid in a black snaky pool in the back garden. I did not know that he was Christ. He was merely a man inexplicably naked. Nakedness had something to do with going on a journey.

There was a piano in the front room, as there seemed to be in all the front rooms of that period, but I never heard my father play it. Elsie did. There was a volume of popular songs that must have been called the *Star Folio*, for there was a star on the cover and a couple dancing. I would take the cat on my knee and sing to it – a rigmarole about dancing on a star. I hear the vowel in 'dancing': the short front one of Manchester. I draw the external world into senseless recitatives: couch dance star cat fire dinner. One Friday my father brought with the weekend joint a large new cash book and a thick-leaded pencil. I began to transfer the external world to its pages in vigorous pictograms. It became a matter of urgency, like going to the lavatory. I saw in some newspaper a heart transfixed by a dart. I had to rush to the cash book and scribble it in before it disappeared.

This early life of fragments has little meaning. There is murk with occasional dull flashes of things and people. It is the lack of continuity that disconcerts, as though one were perpetually dying and being reborn to trivialities. My life as yet had no religion in it. My aunt and cousins were Protestant but did not go to church. My father had probably lost his faith. All his life long he said: 'When you're dead you're finished with.' Nobody taught me how to pray. I do not remember visits from the other Wilsons, who had nothing to mourn and retained a certain devoutness. In 1921 I was taken prematurely to school by little girls who lived two or three doors down. One Friday afternoon I, or they, showed up late. I knew it was Friday, because we had had shop fish and chips for the midday meal, which we called dinner. 'Why are you late, Jack Wilson?' the teacher asked. 'Too many chips,' I said, wondering why I said it. Then we were set to draw a teacup, and the teacher emphasized the slight tapering of its shape. One boy, with modish logicality, drew a perfect inverted cone. I crayoned a multicoloured jack-in-the-box. I think it was a Protestant school, because I half-remember hearing a Protestant hymn sung as the winter twilight settled down. It began 'Herb, hide with me.' Childish religion was full of shadowy characters like Herb. God was Harold on both sides of the fence. His brother Will was cooked till done.

But as yet I had no need of God. My night-time world was terrifying enough without him. Snakes persisted. I remember a dream which may be a distortion of a memory of seeing a film with Mary Pickford in it: she, the young girl, sat on the knee of an old man in a white suit and hat in a garden. They looked calmly at a writhing mass of monsters which prefigured the pythons and hamadryads I was to know in Malaysia. They were all dead white. Where did they come from? I had not at that time been taken to the Belle Vue Zoo. My snakes may have been the Kundalini serpents of the collective unconscious – forms of white female flesh which lived in the base of the spine, already sexual, ready to be transformed into the *prana* or inner life force. They related to bleached dog turds on the road. They were garden worms terrifyingly magnified. A healthy human bowel movement, so I was later to be told in the Royal Army Medical Corps, went 'twice round the pan and was curly at both ends'. The snake as vitalized faeces is still a frightening presence of my dreams. Sometimes I dream that Sigmund Freud and Carl Jung are together, looking at my snakes and coming to no conclusion about them. They have no resemblance to real snakes, which I have found to be graceful, warm, and intelligent. They disappeared from my dreams in Delauneys Road when, after a bout of night hysteria, the picture of the gipsy was removed from my room by my father. But they came back later.

8   Nineteen twenty-two was a key year in modern literature.

It saw the publication of *The Waste Land* and *Ulysses* – a denial of life and a celebration of it. I got out of the waste land of my aunt-mother's house into the vital labyrinth of a huge pub. Nineteen twenty-two was the year of my father's marriage into the Dwyer family. The Dwyers were successful immigrants from Dublin. There was no Irish brogue left in them, and their speech was pure Manchester. The troubles of their native country – the heavy fighting in the capital, with the blowing up of the Four Courts, which followed on the setting up of the Irish Free State in 1921 – aroused little interest. One of the Dwyer women who had stayed behind cursed the curse of Cromwell on the Black and Tans but ended up marrying one of them. Other Dwyers crossed the water later on odd visits, with Irish Sweepstake tickets for illegal sale tucked in their bloomers. The Manchester Dwyers were adoptive Mancunians, though very Catholic in the Irish manner. The greatest member of the family is George Patrick Dwyer, who was to become Bishop of Leeds and then Archbishop of Birmingham. It was he who, in a television discussion, cured Malcolm Muggeridge of his atheism and initiated his long climb to sanctity. When George was installed as archbishop, the novelist Olivia Manning said to me: 'John, I did not realize you were so well connected.' When I told her that Birmingham was merely a Catholic archdiocese, she said: 'Oh, that explains it then.' The economic substructure of the Dwyer passion for turning sons and daughters into 9 bishops and mother superiors was a flourishing greengrocery and poultry business. There was, however, a George Dwyer who went to Australia and became a millionaire. He was involved in sexual irregularities scandalous in a great Catholic family. His son Dan became aide-de-camp to General Blamey.

The woman my father married had herself married into the Dwyers and became one of them. She had been Maggie Byrne, again Manchester Irish, and her husband, Dan Dwyer, had been landlord of the Golden Eagle. She took over the licence when he died – not in the war and not of influenza. She had two grown daughters, Agnes and Madge, of exceptional beauty, though she herself had run to fat in the acceptable mode of pub landladies and suffered from spectacular pains in the feet and back. She was not, in other words, an attractive woman. She was also virtually illiterate and drew her name on a cheque as though from a memory of Egyptian hieroglyphics. Her marrying a Wilson entailed long instruction in the carving of new signs. She needed the strong arm of a husband, whom she called a 'usbint, in the management of a large and rowdy pub in a slum neighbourhood, but the licence was hers, and hers the name in the legal legend over the front door. She was to be boss. My father, once the wedding was over, was bold in rejecting the inferior status proposed and revealed that he had not resigned from Swift's Beef Market. I saw him now even less than previously, and my seclusion in a remote corridor of the labyrinth was perhaps what he sought. He played the piano in the huge music saloon in the evenings, accompanying performers like Tim Carlisle, whose sister Elsie became a famous radio crooner with Ambrose's band. I, as a minor, was not allowed in there, and I was always asleep when the pub closed.

The Golden Eagle of Miles Platting was well known, a boozer of Victorian amplitude, gleaming with brass. The brass sign with its spread wings on the façade was much coveted by local Protestant clergymen. There were three singing rooms, a vast spit-and-sawdust, and a number of snugs. The beer came from the Cornbrook Brewery, which owned the premises and rendered the title landlord or landlady a misnomer. An era of limited drinking hours had been initiated by the Defence of the Realm Act, represented in newspaper cartoons as Dora, a repressive dragon of a female in black, but before the war the pub had opened at six in the morning and did not shut until eleven at night. Workmen came in early for rum and coffee; some came in early and stayed till closing-time. One man died on the premises of delirium tremens, after several days of seeing snakes and Germans leering from the ceiling. There was a legend that an American soldier, not yet demobbed, had come in to boast: 'Waal, I guess and calculate your lil asshole of a country had to call on us to fight your goddam war for you,' and been stabbed to death, his body, by common consent, being deposited in the middle of the night in the middle of

Queen's Road. There was a fearsome character known as Nancy Dickybird, whose violent approach was signalled by runners – 'Nancy's coming.' The main bar would clear on her entrance, and my stepmother would greet her with a truncheon and knuckledusters. There was an extensive armoury available for defence, including two army revolvers complete with ammunition. Nancy would sail into an ecstasy of foulness, urinate on the floor, and then leave.

Lodge Street was a tough street in a tough area. I had moved a short way south from my birthplace to the northern segment of Miles Platting, with Collyhurst to the west, but the Queen's Road where my mother had shopped was the tram-clanging artery which fed all these districts. I was in an ugly world with ramshackle houses and foul back alleys, not a tree or a flower to be seen, though Queen's Park and a general cemetery were available to the north-west if a breath of green was required. If the beer-intake of an urban area is an index of its prosperity, then Miles Platting was not badly off, but heavy patronage of the Golden Eagle often meant neglect of domestic responsibilities. A husband came into the public bar one evening in need of his pint. He was shaken. His wife, dead out from a debauch with her cronies, had left the bathing of the children to him. He conscientiously sluiced them all in a tin tub, dressed them for bed, then asked one girl: 'Where's your nightdress, love?' The girl said: 'I don't live here.' It was a district where the women did most of the fighting, usually because of suspected or discovered adultery. For a small transgression, it was enough to smash the delinquent's downstairs windows with a house key. But in bar or street or alley there could be hair-tearing and even breast-slashing. Children played barefoot not because they had no shoes but because they had grown out of them.

The old Lancashire mythology of clogs and shawls and morning knocker-up was to be looked for now more in towns like Rochdale than in Manchester districts like Miles Platting. The clatter of clogs was infrequent, but black shawls were plentiful. My stepmother and stepsisters put them on when they went shopping. The knocker-up was dying out because of the advent of cheap alarm-clocks. My Uncle Billy had once taunted an old woman knocker-up with her long pole that could tap at upper windows: 'Hallo, missis, art going fishing?' He was chased and swiped with 'I'll give you fishing, you young bugger.' It was he who had given the lying excuse for being late for work one summer morning: 'I slept with my pillow on the window sill. Knocker-up knocked pillow and I couldn't hear.'

I was brought to the Golden Eagle without warning of what was in store for me. There was no attempt to prepare me for a change of ménage. I was brought into the pub by my father between three o'clock closing and five-thirty reopening, trod sawdust and tried to take in brass beer engines and swabbing barmen, then toddled left down a corridor to a bright kitchen-living-room where the three 13 females of my new life were waiting for me. They had not seen me before. I wanted my mother. 'This is your mother now, love, and these are your sisters. Her you called your mother is now your Auntie Annie.' I was thin, small, pale, undernourished. Annie, my new mother said, had done her best but it hadn't been good enough. As an earnest of a more nutritious regime she handed me a fairy cake. I knocked it out of her hand. The younger daughter, Madge, said, without rancour: 'You'll be buried with your hand sticking up out of the grave, and everybody that passes by will hit it and say: There lies the boy that knocked a fairy cake out of his mother's hand.' My stepmother should have swiped me but did not. She was pretty tolerant. The introduction of a snivelling lad into her household meant a new gratuitous responsibility, and she had a pub to run. I was to sleep in the little downstairs room of Harry the chief and resident barman, on a little trucklebed. Shortly afterwards a proper child's bed was bought for me, and it was placed in the corner of the master bedroom where my father and his new wife slept. I have no recollection of waking up to amorous noises.

I remember going to bed in the summer light, unable to sleep because of the downstairs racket. I wandered that upper floor, which, corresponding to the ground-floor drinking palace, was vast and had a huge drawing-room with eight windows looking down on Lodge Street and one of its slummy tributaries. I would go into all the bedrooms

and micturate in all the chamberpots. I would return to the
drawing-room and try to leave some residuary golden drops
on the carpet. Then I would bang the piano. Nobody heard.
Down below three pianos thumped and tinkled simul-
taneously, like something by Charles Ives. Across the road
from the window by my bed a gramophone played 'Margie'
or 'The Holy City'. I looked out of another window, which
dominated an outdoor women's lavatory and its yard. One
black-shawled crone said to another. 'He sent me this letter,
the false bastard.' And she showed it before taking it into
the closet to befoul.

My stepmother, whatever else she was, was a good plain
cook, skilled at mutton stews, meat and potato pies, classical
hotpots, fruit tarts, nutmeggy custards. My fattening began
with butties spread with home-made damson jam. Breakfast
was bacon and a fried egg, with bacon fat poured all over
the plate: this was for the dipping of bread and was called
dip. I ate but was perpetually angry. I expressed my anger in
drawings of my stepmother wearing a chef's toque, beating a
pudding batter, and displaying male genitals. These were
the only genitals I knew about, and I always scrawled the
penis as an icon of foul insult. I lacked the comforting
contact of female flesh, and when I was offered it by my
stepsisters I was unwilling to accept it. I would be called
into their bedroom in the morning while they were dressing
and told to give them 'a kiss and a love', but I was shy of
touching their exposed arms and backs. They noted the

shyness and giggled at it. They were well-shaped girls with fine Irish creamy flesh, a year or so between them, in their very early twenties. Agnes was coal-haired and showed the blood of a wrecked Armada; Madge was prettily mousy. They were pure and deeply Catholic. They took me to mass, which was boring and incomprehensible, but the Gregorian line of a priest (the mass must have been high and sung) stuck in my head: '*Per omnia saecula saeculorum.*' A queer kind of English, a sort of code, the *orum* dangerous magic.

I was a fidgety child, and, as a revenge for my transplanting, fidgeted odd coins off the kitchen dresser into my pockets. I see myself, fidgety, being told to lie still on the kitchen sofa, the pub cat in my arms, while the two-minute silence of November 11, 1922 was observed. If I moved, I was told, the war would start again. I did not know what the war was, but one-legged drinkers in the public bar, men coughing their lungs up, black boozing widows were the war. War was a word like 'runcible' or a termination like *orum*. In November my stepmother started mixing her Christmas puddings. In December the greengrocer-poulterer Dwyers arrived with the colossal turkey. On Christmas Day, when the licensing hours imitated Sunday, the pub closed at two and Christmas dinner was eaten at three. The turkey stuffing was herbs and pork sausage meat. No Dwyers came for Christmas, nor any Byrnes. My stepmother and her brother had quarrelled, as always happens in families, over a family will. The Dwyers kept their own green Christmas over the greengrocer's shop, laden with all the unsold holly and mistletoe, but the Wilsons were welcome at the Golden Eagle. My stepmother approved of my two uncles – the master plumber Jack, who looked like Stanley Baldwin, the common plumber Jimmy, who looked like James Maxton and whose wife Lily, my apparent godmother, she considered a shiftless slut.

My grandfather was dead by 1922, and my grandmother kept to her bed in a rented house with an imported pair of Finnegan girls to look after her. My father had taken me to visit her by tram – a clean, smiling old Irish lady sitting up in a lace mobcap – and I had begun to learn to read on the outward and homeward journeys, my primer my father's packet of Three Castles with its citation from Thackeray's *The Virginians*: 'There's no sweeter tobacco than comes from Virginia, and no finer brand than the Three Castles.' I was seeing more of my father now. He had even lifted me from sleep to be shown to some visitors in that huge drawing-room. I remember crying: 'Bugger off, you buggers,' at the same time wondering where I had learned the word and its double usage. It came from nowhere, like the chef's toque and the genital obscenity.

The visiting Wilsons were two families. My Uncle Jack and Aunt Nell spoke grammatical Lancashire English, as befitted a master plumber and his wife, and their two daughters, Joan and Winifred (who was later to sign her name Wynné), were to be taught the piano. My Uncle Jimmy and 17

Aunt Lily had the one daughter, named for my dead sister Muriel. She was to become a dancer with stage hopes, but she declined into being a hostess in a night club run by a former boxer. The Wilsons were revealed as a fair-haired family, except for Uncle Jimmy, who had picked up a Spanish swarthiness and Eskimo straight hair. My father and Uncle Jack were gingerish. My cousins were pale of eyelash and had translucent skins. I was to favour my Uncle Jimmy in a modified form – hair curly and dark brown, near-invisible eyebrows a half-hearted tribute to the family fairness. The family nose was assertive. '*Il est juif, sans doute*,' a French lady said of me in 1939, in a Luxembourg night club full of visiting Nazis.

These Christmas parties, beginning in the Golden Eagle, continued in the later locales to which we moved. After the afternoon torpor there was the powerful tea of my stepmother and rich iced volcanic-earth-coloured uneatable Christmas cake. The real festivities began after ten at night, when my cousins and myself were dropped food-drugged and bloated into the one double bed. There was a supper of cold turkey and ham and tongue with piccalilli, sherry trifle, charlotte russe, mince pies, the sullen reappearance of the Christmas cake, Moët et Chandon champagne. Then in the great drawing-room three pianists accompanied songs in turn – my father, my Aunt Nell, my stepsister Madge. The songs were 'Finnegan's Ball', 'Here's Another One Off To America', 'Coronation Day' (the correct version, not

Buck Mulligan's), 'Pale Hands I Loved', 'Because', 'Dear Little Shamrock', numbers from *Little Nelly Kelly*, 'Ma, He's Making Eyes At Me', 'Avalon', 'Yes, We Have No Bananas'. When my cousins and I had grown, and another pair of cousins had been added to the master plumber's ménage, we too participated, and I sang 'The Golden Vanity' with, for some reason, my trousers falling down. Trousers were called kex, which properly means the dry hollow stalk of umbellifers like cow parsnip and wild chervil.

Clad in new short kex, I was taken to school in 1923, to St Edmund's RC Elementary at the corner of Monsall Road and Upper Monsall Street. I was still weak and unmuscular through having no proper mother, though I was no longer undernourished. In the school hall, Miss Sullivan, the headmistress, a dried spinster of ferocious irritability now rarely seen in schools, ordered us to crawl in a phalanx like little mice, and I see myself still as a lone mouse laggard, all the others well ahead. There were, till the tropics ruined them, photographs of me at six, one of them as a melancholy pierrot, and the pallor under the straight fringe, the deficient vitality, the rejection of the external world were striking and terrible. But I could read fluently, apparently without much teaching. Miss O'Flaherty wrote THE CAT SAT ON THE MAT on the blackboard, and I was the only one in the class able to rattle it off, though, through a kind of surrealist perverseness more than ignorance, I transposed the nouns. Miss O' Flaherty had a short way with chatterers. She would

19

make them stand in front of the class and paste over their mouths, using gloy from the conical gloypot, a neatly scissored strip of coloured paper. One boy, a sufferer from adenoid growths ('Dodt do it, biss, I cadt breathe') screamed at the prospect and fainted. Another boy, tall and with a courtly manner, accepted the punishment philosophically. When Miss O'Flaherty was not looking, he doffed the gag, smiled and bowed, then replaced it. It was better than the strap from Miss Sullivan.

I was now taught some Catholicism, which chiefly had to do with eternal punishment for trivial offences. We were told that each of us had a guardian angel, an invisible monitor even in the lavatory, and we sang a song to him or her or it:

> Guardian angel, from heaven so bright,
> Watching beside me to keep me aright,
> Fold thy wings round me and guard me with love,
> Softly sing songs to me of heav'n above.
> Beautiful angel, so tender and mild,
> Lovingly guard me, for I am thy child.

It was a harmless and charming fiction; it still is. But the Manichee in us all, even at the age of six, had to assume that there was another angel, a very bad one, hitting out at the pale epicene from heaven, and, since fighting was a sin, winning most of the rounds. One of our teachers, more Butlerian than was right for a Catholic, assured us that sins like nose-picking and incontinence of the bladder were really a disease that merited our being carted off to Monsall Isolation Hospital, which was just across the road. Presumably people were cut up there in isolation. I was sent there eventually, but it was for scarlet fever.

To be a Catholic meant primarily belonging to a minority faction which was despised by the scholars of St Augustine's C of E Elementary School, on the other side of Monsall Street. I was taught by my fellows to call them proddy dogs in response to their jeer of cat licks. The opposed canticles of abuse are still going strong in Northern Ireland.

> Cat lick, cat lick, going to mass,
> Riding to hell on the devil's ass

was answered by

> Proddy dog, proddy dog on the wall,
> A small raw spud will feed you all.
> A ha'penny candle will give you light
> To read the Bible of a Sunday night.

I did not know what the Bible was, but evidently it was a dirty book. It was confirmed for me later that not only was it dirty, it was dangerous. It was the prime cause of people losing their Catholic faith. This is, historically speaking, a sound enough judgement. There was perturbation at my secondary school when the Book of Job was a set book for the Higher School Certificate examination. My English teacher, a Xaverian brother who had not read it before, 21 conceded that the style was sound even if the theology was shaky. Anyway, the Bible was mostly a foul book that had produced proddy dogs.

Across the street from the Golden Eagle was a little shop run by the Misses Hogan, a couple of witches in dusty black. After two days of constipation I was sent across there with a teacup to buy two pennyworth of California syrup of figs. This, the most saccharine thing, outside the films of Mary Pickford, that California ever produced, did not act at once but when it did act it acted relentlessly. I was taken short in afternoon school and bewrayed my kex shamefully. In the whole of a man's life there is no worse humiliation than the dropping of that heavy load clothed. I had to run home, accompanied by two girls, and was given by Madge for some reason a lace doily for the tersive act. I was in a deep pit of shame, but my schoolfellows, when I went back next morning in fresh kex digesting a hardboiled egg, did not point the finger. It was the sort of thing that might happen to anyone, like being bust. 'You see that lad over there? Well, he's bust.' This meant that in the playground the one remaining button at the back of his kex had snapped off. One lad to whom it happened said: 'Told my bloody mother to sew the bloody thing on proper and she didn't bloody listen. Now my bloody kex is coming bloody down. Have to walk bloody home with my bloody hands in my bloody pockets, bloody it. And there goes the blooming bell.'

There were certain school clowns who, for a halfpenny

fee, would guarantee to make you laugh. One boy had a continuing saga about a man with a dog called Bugger. The two were always travelling by rail. The guard would shout 'All change for Oldham,' and the man would say: 'Come on, Bugger, we're on the wrong train again.' On the way home from school, one little girl pointed me out to her friend as a boy that could make you laugh. I obliged with funny faces and no fee charged. The faces were funny only in the sense that they were the objective correlative of an exercise of the risor muscles. Nature was telling these children to laugh, and it would have been madness to laugh at nothing. There is nothing intrinsically funny in anything – certainly not in a man whose dog was named Bugger. One regular comedian of St Edmund's would exchange humour for cigarette cards, but he had to be given the cards first. The cards were his comic property. He would hold them up to the sun and say: 'You see them? Them's shit, them is. Ta-ta.' And he would amble off, his act finished, occasionally turning round with his tongue lolling as we collapsed in dutiful mirth. The performance was highly popular. Young learners about sex are told nowadays that an orgasm is a kind of sneeze. Laughter is the same kind of shocked release but it is less apocalyptical and, to most children, pleasurably controllable, like the action of the rectal sphincter. When I published my first novel, I was surprised to be told it was comic. Those two little girls were making a proleptic judgement on my career.

At the age of six a social function was imposed upon me that had everything to do with entertainment, though not necessarily of the comic kind. On Queen's Road there were two cinemas – the Rex and the Electric. They faced each other, like the Globe and the Rose playhouses on the Elizabethan South Bank, but not in true rivalry. Going to one on a Monday and Thursday (the day the programme changed) did not prevent your going to the other on a Tuesday and Friday, if you could afford it. The cinemagoer's criteria had more to do with hygiene than with the quality of the entertainment offered. The Rex was called a bughouse and the Electric not. The Electric used a superior disinfectant like a grudging perfume; the Rex smelt of its patrons and its lavatories. With the Rex, it was said, you went in in a blouse and came out with a jumper. So it was to the Electric that the children of Lodge Street went, clutching their pennies, on a Saturday afternoon. Because I lived at the Golden Eagle I was called Jackie Eagle, and ten or twelve boys would, after midday dinner, cry out for Jackie Eagle from the verge of the public bar the law forbade them to enter. They would hold on to me in their redolent jerseys all the way down Lodge Street and left and over on Queen's Road. I was the only one of them who could read.

The manager of the Electric did not wish too many even of his front rows to be defiled by children, and so we were jammed three to a seat, with a gaping black auditorium behind us clean for the evening's two houses. So I began a lifetime's devotion to the cinema, a one-sided love affair in which I was more bruised than caressed. In those old silent days the art was almost an aspect of literature. I heard my little treble voice crying the text aloud for the benefit of even big louts whom the reading mystery had passed by. 'Kiss me, my fool,' mouths the Spanish gipsy siren, and the caballero who proposed knifing her trembles so that his knife silently clatters to the floor. 'Came the dawn,' a regular cliché. We saw Rudolph Valentino in *The Sheik* and Ben Turpin in *The Shriek*. There was *The Four Horsemen of the Apocalypse* ('What's that mean, kid?'), with artistic camera-masks that varied the shape of the frame. There was a Chester Conklin comedy which began with lovers kissing on a doorstep. 'The end,' the legend said. There were roars of kids cheated. 'Of a perfect day.' That was all right, then, but the humour was too adult for relief: the buggers were clearly not to be trusted. There was one frightful shock for me. A character with dirty beard and gabardine spoke, and then the black screen filled with unintelligible letters. I know now it was Hebrew; I even remember a beth and a ghimel. To my illiterates it was all one, and there was bafflement and then anger at my failure to twang it off. 'Thought you said the bugger could read.' So I improvised a flight of suitable invective. No piano played in the pit: we were too cheap for music.

At Christmas 1923 my stepsisters took me to the panto-mime at the Palace Theatre on Oxford Street in the heart   25 of the city. It was *Dick Whittington* and Dorothy Ward was the principal boy. She sang 'Nothing Could Be Finer Than To Be In Carolina In The Mor-or-orning'. This was theatre, this was the real thing. The auditorium smelt of cigars and rustled with chocolate boxes. Dick and his cat soared over us in a balloon. When I got back to the family kitchen I was hysterical with wonder at the size of the proscenium arch. 'It stretched from there to there,' and I ran with trembling pointing arm from one end of the kitchen to the other. The mensuration was sound in a relative way: one kind of architectural extension was the figure of another. Dorothy Ward's song summed up the magic and still does. Where was Carolina? In America, like California. Where is America? Never mind. Carolina must have been better than California: it exported no bewraying syrup of figs. When I first went to Chapel Hill in North Carolina I found I remembered every word of the song and could even play it on the piano. 'If I had Aladdin's lamp for only a day, I'd make a wish, and here's what I'd say: Nothing could be finer than . . .'

The years become confused, obedient to Proust or Ford Madox Ford. Real time emerges with a vague chronology. I could not have been sitting in the front porch of the Golden Eagle in the enchanted days after seeing *Dick Whittington*, trying to draw a stage on a panel of a shoebox. ('What's that you're drawing, kid?' – 'A pantomime.' – 26 'You're bloody daft.') It must have been in the spring of

1924. But I get up from my work and toddle to the kitchen, where the women are discussing the scandal of Fatty Arbuckle, a muffled news item of 1923, which gave California a worse name than syrup of figs, or the wedding of the Duke and Duchess of York, which, as the Queen Mother will confirm, took place on April 26 of that year. I can recall no procession of the seasons, which Lodge Street could not manifest through flowery spring or russet autumn. I can remember no rain, and rain, according to the outsider's myth of Manchester, is the one thing I ought to remember. I seem to have spent a lot of time sitting in fine weather in the porch of the Golden Eagle, drawing or else playing with the sixpenny toys I could buy at the Misses Hogan's — metal fishes to be fished for with a magnetic rod, a fragile carthbound Sopwith Camel. Also reading.

The reading must have reached a fair stage of efficacy before the Saturday processions to the Electric. I had a weekly paper for children called *Chick's Own*, with Rupert the Chick as the front-page hero. This came out on Mondays. Madge said that *Tiger Tim's Weekly*, out on Thursdays, was a nice paper too, and it sounded sympathetic. I was called a weakly child, and it was comforting to think of a tiger brought down to my level. I read the balloons in the cartoons about anthropomorphic animals, and assumed that the print récit under the coloured pictures would be beyond me. But it was not: I was merely lazy. Words were helpfully split with hyphens into their constitu- 27 ent morphemes. There was always a full-page story that did not so condescend. This I found I could read too. 'Let us give this poor dog some of our hot soup.' 'Soup' I read as 'soap', not unreasonably, since that is how it is rendered in what Henry Higgins calls Broad Romic. The notion of comforting with hot soap was not unpleasant. Soap was at least wholesome – the whole of Miles Platting, said my stepmother, could do with more of it – and might be palatable hot.

The wicked press barons who put out these twopenny rations of kidfeed had sensible editors. The child's ideal companion would be a rational animal with his own weaknesses. Animals will take love without demanding it; they have teeth, but they will not bite with the vindictiveness of human adults. They are free and indifferent, but they will go into spasms of affection with a discontinuity the child understands. They demand no covenant and do not know the meaning of obligation. Dress them in jerseys and kex, give them a minimal vocabulary but no expressiveness in their masks, save the query marks of an occasional smile of triumph at some naughtiness, and they earn love without mawkishness. I look back at that anonymous sub-art with a genuine gratitude. I saw no implausibility in Porkyboy's eating sausages for Christmas breakfast or Tiger Tim making a stew out of bread and cheese. The gentle way out of the animal world into the human was through Marzipan the Magician, with his candy-striped wand, and the gnome

Bushybeard. Stories about human adults would have been frightening, for human adults were irrational, gross, demanding. They also rejected magic, whose power had been confirmed by the child's distortion of religion. Certain features in both of my weaklies or weeklies encouraged, like a gentle laxative, activities which would have been too costively painful in school. You became numerate through linking digits with a pencil and ending with an angular cartoon sketch. You could paste a torso and sundered limbs on a piece of card, scissor them out and assemble them with paper fasteners, so that you had a flat marionette that could walk and gesture. These publications had an acceptable moral content. Naughtiness was behovely, but all would be well.

Incoming and outgoing customers must have noted something unhealthy in this thin-legged child drawing on ragged card or gaping over *Chick's Own*. I should have been throwing stones or kicking an old tennis ball about Lodge Street with its tougher urchins, or slopping in bare feet through the mud and horse-merds. Occasionally, to oblige, I would take off my shoes and half-heartedly slop, only to have my shoes stolen. That was naughty. My stepmother would take time off from the beer pumps to clout me. I would cry and be called, as D. H. Lawrence had been called, mardarse. The clouting would then be just enough, but there was a double clouting that was not. There was a hired girl named Bertha, who turned out to be mad. She came down the stairs that led from the private quarters to the sawdust concourse that was the public bar. It was a noble staircase, and she descended with the grace of a Tolstoy princess. But she was stark naked. She had to be taken back to her parents in Collyhurst. Clothed, of course. Before then she had played on me a trick of curious malice. Every Monday we children had to take to school a coin in an envelope, a contribution to an African mission for dragging black infants to the light. I took my wrapped penny, but it turned out to be a penny-sized watch crystal. I was clouted in class and then clouted when I took home a written complaint. Bertha eventually admitted with glee that she had been responsible for the pointless substitution, but by then it was too late. The great truth of the world's injustice had been established for me.

A strange collective naughtiness came over a group of us when we were going back to school one day after the dinner break. A ragged man appeared from an alley, which was called also an entry or a ginnel, with a battered straw hat set rakishly. He danced and played a tin whistle. He was a pied piper whom we had to follow. He also sang the songs of the day – 'Margie' and 'I'm Forever Blowing Bubbles'. We joined in, we capered, we followed him from street to street. Then he doffed his cady in farewell and disappeared down another entry. We were very late for school, but, because the piper was an undoubted adult, we had felt him

somehow to be a representative of the establishment that

regulated our education, a kind of demented school inspector. We were not walloped by Miss Sullivan: there were too many of us. There was also a sinister magic in the occasion which she must have recognized. There was a mystery to be considered: the cane did not meet the case.

My joining a group of peers, delinquent or not, was a rarity. I was grasped eagerly, even desperately, on Saturday afternoons, when the eccentricity of my being able to read was a blessing, but for the rest of the time I was either distractedly persecuted or ignored. On Saturday mornings I would stroll like a clubman down Lodge Street, turn right on Queen's Road and go into an ice cream parlour that served a penny vanilla ice in a glass dish. I was cut off from the halfpenny wafer-lickers. I was Jackie Eagle, who partook of the glory of the polished brass effigy with its spread pinions, of the wet wealth within. I was also one despised, mardarse.

In 1924 there was a change in my life. My stepmother grew tired of the stress of what she called the public business, and my father had had enough of Swift's Beef Market. It was time his book-keeping skills were employed to a more profitable end. The stock and goodwill of the Golden Eagle were sold to a new tenant, and we moved to a tobacconist's shop on Princess Road, Moss Side. This was a sizeable migration.

Moss Side, which was to become a Caribbean slum, was at that time a respectable district with decent houses, front gardens with trees in them, a bowling green, the scent of a coming seediness. It was a long way south from Queen's Road. The small boy who could reduce the stage of the Palace Theatre ('Butterflies will flutter up and kiss each little buttercup at daw-aw-awning') to the dimensions of the Golden Eagle kitchen could as easily expand a city to a world. Harpurhey and Miles Platting were now wrapped in north-eastern cold, and the bulk of Ancoats, the city centre itself, the University and Hulme kept off the Arctic winds. Moss Side is bounded by Moss Lane East and West to the north. Princess Road is to its east. In my boyhood it ran north through Hulme to the centre, as it does still, but to the south it stopped at Southern Cemetery. It was to move on to new housing estates like Wythenshawe and lead to the international airport at Ringway. Princess Road was like Queen's Road, a loud artery which fed quieter streets. These considered the impropriety of becoming slums before leafy Moss Lane East banished the thought. Trams clanged down and up Princess Road, and one of my first sights there was of an amorous dog caught in a cowcatcher. Our shop was Number 21, and Wilson's stood in gold paint over its window. The name did not represent my father's new assertiveness. It was also my stepmother's now, and M. Wilson was inked like an ideogram at the foot of cheques. Our shop was divided by a narrow alley or entry from a cinema called the Palace. On the other side of the shop was a barber, Louis Cohen. The cinema was run by Jakie Innerfield. Jews thus entered my life, admirably flamboyant ones. Innerfield had come south from Cheetham Hill, the Jewish quarter very well presented in Louis Golding's forgotten novel *Magnolia Street*. Innerfield's two daughters were Jewesses of a recognizably Cheetham Hill type – dark, scented, overdressed, dangerously erotic. Manchester Jewish speech seemed strongly adenoidal and always loud. Manchester Jews matched Manchester Catholics by getting on. They recognized an affinity.

The shop sold not only cigarettes and tobacco but boxes of chocolates: it was not a sweet shop in the sense that you could buy gobstoppers or Ogo–Pogo sticks there. Ogo–Pogo sticks were named for a mythical creature in a popular song:

> I'm looking for the Ogo-Pogo,
> The funny little Ogo-Pogo.
> His father was an earwig,
> His mother was a whale.
> I want to put a little bit of salt on his tail.

Though customers could come in for a packet of Player's or Gold Flake or Black Cat, the business was from the first trying to expand into a wholesale supply depot for smaller shops. Rough boys coming to buy their fathers a packet of Woodbines would see me proudly lifting the heavy wooden slab that was a continuation of the counter. 'You're not supposed to go in there, kid,' they would say. But I could 33 say: 'I live here.' Beyond the shelves crammed with King George V and Gold Leaf chocolates, and cigarettes, some of them of brands now forgotten, lay the stockroom. Here parcels were made up for delivery by a straw-haired young man named Harold Smith. He taught me a song:

> I want to be alone,
> Yes, I want to be alone,
> I want to be alone with Mary Brown.
> Would I take her through the park?
> Yes, I'd kiss her in the dark
> And tell her she's the nicest girl in town.
> Is she a raving beauty?
> No, I wouldn't call her that.
> Has she a form like Venus?
> No, she's just a trifle fat.
> But she's got a lot of dough
> And she's single now, you know.
> So I want to be alone with Mary Brown.

The stockroom had a strong odour of the pinewood of Swan matches and it was full of huge cartons, some empty. Harold Smith shut me in one of these and then sat on the flaps. I learned fear of darkness and asphyxiation. I think of dying even now as being shut in an empty cardboard carton. It is the panic of not being able to breathe that affects many Mancunians. The damp air, admirable for cotton spinning, brings us up bronchial. One of my earliest medicines for a weak chest was Owbridge's Lung Tonic, which had once contained opium. There were other opiates, all from the North-West – Battley's Sedative Solution, Dover's Powder, Dr Collis Browne's Chlorodyne, Godfrey's Cordial, Mrs Winslow's Soothing Syrup, Atkinson's Infants' Preservative, Street's Infant's Quietness. We needed opium up there, but doctors' lobbyings had banned it. It was at 21 Princess Road that I first became aware of Manchester's damp. It had never rained on Lodge Street; it was all reserved for Moss Side.

Behind the stockroom was a small living-dining-room at whose table my father kept the books and looked after the orders. He always wore a bowler hat while working, and he had a fine heavy ebony ruler of the kind that Bob Cratchit raises to the Scrooge whose new benevolence looks like madness. It was a dark room looking on to Louis Cohen's backyard, and the electric light was always on. Beyond it was the kitchen where my stepmother cooked. I saw more of her now, and of my father, though it was mainly his waistcoated back and his bowler, which he called a pot. My stepmother watched him at his figure-totting as though he would cheat her. But he had only an actuarial control of the money: it was she who carried the account at Williams Deacon's Bank at the corner of Princess Road and Moss Lane East.

She revealed herself now as interested mainly in money, not so much the acquisition of it as the fear of losing it. Had she done the right thing in leaving the public? Was my father competent to conserve her capital? She had little to do now but cook and brood, teeing and laying as she put it while she lay sleepless in bed. Agnes and Madge were working, both of them at the Manchester offices of Famous Lasky, which organized the distribution of Paramount pictures through the North-West. They were both courting, and soon they would marry, and there was the question of the cost of their weddings. My stepmother talked of little but her pains and apprehension about money. She was interested in other people's pains, though more pharmaceutically than compassionately, for she had a number of home-made remedies inherited from her misty Irish past. These were dangerous and contained paregoric, ipecacuanha, and a substance she called ikey-pikey. My father, given a cloudy bottle for his cough, would hide it unopened in a drawer. She made me gargle with chloride of lime. To comb one's hair with water was good for it. After all, the hair was a plant, and plants throve on water. When, run down and weak as I was, I got blood-poisoning in my left leg through carrying a pen with a rusty nib in my stocking, she exacerbated the poison with hot fomentations. But she cooked well and gave us all a fine shop tea of tinned salmon, lettuce with Lazenby's dressing, and cream horns from Price's up the street. 'Eat hearty,' she would say. 'There's half a crown's worth of food on the table.'

Upstairs was the drawing-room, with a piano hardly touched by my father. The room was used for alternate courting by the two daughters. There was a portable gramophone up there, with Layton and Johnstone ready to sing 'It Ain't Gonna Rain No More' and 'Bye Bye, Blackbird'. There was also 'Me And Jane In A Plane', played by Jack Hilton's Orchestra, and, on the other side, 'I'm Going Back To Imazaz (Imazaz the pub next door)'. Why does one remember these vapidities so well?

> I'll be keeping my eye
> On the man in the moon.
> He's a dangerous guy
> When he starts to spoon.
> My kisses I'll shower
> A million an hour.
> No traffic cop
> Will ever stop
> Me and Jane in a plane.

Open on the piano was a new song which Madge played and sang. It was called 'When It's Nighttime In Italy It's Wednesday Over Here'. One of the lines ran: 'Oh, the onions in Sicily make people cry in California.' So they ought to cry, the bewraying buggers. I would take no more of their syrup of figs.

We had also a crystal set, a miracle never superseded by electronics, for music and speech of insuperable clarity came from a cat's whisker tickling a tiny nugget of carborundum pyrites. 2ZY was the Manchester call sign. We heard John Henry and Blossom. And also 'If you speak to an Eskimo his breath will freeze your ear. When it's night-time in Italy –' And then the patch of crystal would die and a new facet had to be tickled. My father was not impressed by the wonder. The only entertainment he sought was in the Alexandra Hotel, a pub opposite Williams Deacon's Bank. There he drank draught Bass with new cronies, most of them shopkeepers like himself – Lee and Aldridge, rival butchers; Price, floury and vanilla-scented from the cake shop; Flynn, smelling of fish; the manager of Seymour Meads, who looked like an undertaker; an undertaker. I saw more of him, but not much.

Visits from the Wilsons were, as before, reserved for Christmas, but the greengrocer Dwyers – Jack and Ima – came with a professional interest in the new shopkeeping venture. Other relatives, and relatives of relatives, turned up for Sunday tea. There was even a German relative of relatives named Wilhelm Froelich but called Billy Fraylish, Catholic Bavarian and headmaster of a Catholic elementary school. He told coarse jokes in a full-blooded Manchester accent. 'Why does the sea roar?' – 'Wouldn't you roar if you had crabs on your bottom?' I remained unsociable, too much the silent reader of *Chick's Own* and *Tiger Tim's Weekly*. A weakly child still, not enough devilment.

The school I was sent to was the Bishop Bilsborrow Memorial Elementary up Princess Road, next to the tram
depot. Because of its religious liaison with the English Mar-

tyrs Church on Alexandra Road, which was the near parallel of Princess Road, it was sometimes itself called the English Martyrs. Nobody knew who Bishop Bilsborrow was, beside presumably being an English martyr. I have never found out. Bilsborrow sounded like bilberry, and the Protestant children called us Ripe English Tomaters: there was a flavour of Dwyer greengrocery around. We were told what martyrs were – Catholics mostly Irish unbelievably tortured by the English proddy dogs. This was to habituate us to the tortures meted out by Sister Ignatius, the headmistress. She raised the strap back over her shoulder before smiting. She never missed.

I was too young for her. I was with Mother Andrea, who looked after the juniors. I rose from the first class to the second in half an hour, being the only one who could read, with noise and fluency, the neat print script on the black-board: 'Stop, stop, Mr Pancake. But the pancake went spinning like a wheel down the hill.' Mother Andrea had a sweet face and was kind and gentle. She taught us the Our Father and the Hail Mary and the Glory Be. We knew who Hail Mary was. There was a statue of her, in blue with a wreath of stars, in the school hall. There older boys, whose screams from the strap we could hear, were sent sobbing to kneel and beg forgiveness. We had to be satisfied with the promise of more apocalyptical punishments. Hell, gently explained by Mother Andrea, was all the more terrible for the gentleness. 'For ever, Mother Andrea?' – 'Yes, for ever and ever. 39

I pray to Almighty God that none of you children will ever merit his eternal fire.' The End of the World might not be far off. It might come so swiftly that sinners would not have time to repent.

One summer's day the End of the World came. A sunny morning grew, in an instant, black. It was industrial fog, encouraged by the rare lack of a western wind to settle. The classroom lights were switched on: it was the middle of the night before dinnertime. It may also, said Mother Andrea gently, be the consummation of all things. Let us pray. The prayer was efficacious. God relented. A summer's day returned to sinful Manchester. But it had been a terrible moment.

I fell in love with a girl named Joan Price. She was dark, pretty, probably of Silurian stock, and she was seven years old like myself. I fell in love with her because she was talented. She could sing 'Felix Kept On Walking' with a stylized lope, hands joined behind in the manner of Pat Sullivan's cartoon character, whom we all knew and admired in both his animated and syndicated strip forms. She was sometimes asked to perform during one of the little dancing lessons we were given when Mother Andrea was oppressed by the tedium of Sums. My love for her was expressed through the urge to make her admire her admirer through skill in her own sphere. I offered to sing the whole of 'Me And Jane In A Plane' but did not get past these lines:

In my two-seater
What could be sweeter?
I'll have St Peter
Step inside
And bless the bride.

They were considered blasphemous. 'Proddy dog,' jeered some classmates. Joan Price was our only star. I loved her without knowing what love was. Not having yet read William Blake, I told my love, though not to my love, and discovered that the rest of the boys knew what love was. Love was kissing. In the playground a gang tried to force us to kiss. The mask of fury of a girl can be terrifyingly adult. Joan Price beat me with her hard little fists. I learned, and have never unlearned, that falling in love is dangerous.

One humiliation followed another. I found that I was colour blind. That could be called a kind of unwilled patriotism, since John Dalton, after whom the complaint is named in most languages, discovered its existence while teaching at New College, Manchester. I was already known to be able to draw well, but my first trial with water paints had me making green leaves orange. My classmates saw first with awe and then with giggles, and they called on others to see and giggle. They were in the presence not of decent stupidity, like getting a sum wrong; this was a physical deformity. Mother Andrea was not teaching us; a Miss Clayton, later to be called Clayballs by her pupils, had come down from the upper school to give us what was called Art.

The crowd around my desk attracted her. She came, saw, and hit. It was a response pedagogically unsound. She shook me before the class and held up my painting for derision. She, or I, got plenty of that.

They say that about one in fifty of males is daltonian. It is a defect of the optic nerve passed on from grandfather to grandson through the female, who is rarely colour blind herself. Apparently it is due to the absence of one of the photopigments in the foveal cones. The Ishihara test shows me to have a particularly full-blooded variety of the defect. There is a kind of *pointilliste* diagram crammed with polychrome dots: a large white 2 appears in it for the normally endowed; for the daltonians there is a large white unequivocal 5. But for me there is more than a dubiety about green and the various reds, or blue and violet. I am not sure how to name any colour; I am totally without a chromatic glossary. I recognize that there is a huge variety of colours in the world, but I am dubious about saying what they are. Women, who cannot understand the defect, like to test me with their gamboges and aubergines, and end in awe, as in the presence of genius. Women, anyway, have a wider colour vocabulary than men, and no man ought to turn his back on John Dalton as on the prophet of a breed of cripples. There is more colour blindness around than is recognized.

I make a plea for the daltonians to all organizations that use a colour taxonomy on the oppository lines of a phonemic system. At Charles-de-Gaulle airport in Paris, travellers to the United States are split up for boarding on the basis of the issue of a card of a colour of perverse subtlety, as befits the capital of *haute couture* – violet, vermilion, kelly green. There are concert halls with green areas and brown areas. If the three colours of traffic signals were displaced I should be lost. There is sympathy for the blind, but not for the colour blind. There is also an epistemological problem. If a daltonian reads green as orange, what philosopher may say that he is wrong? The secondary realities, of which colour is one, are not to be decreed by a majority vote.

Clearly, daltonianism is a barrier to the writing of fiction (less, it would seem, to the painting of pictures, where the bizarrely idiosyncratic vision may be accepted. Turner? Cézanne?). Fiction deals with the external world, where things are coloured, and the fiction-writer has to get the colours right. My first wife not only used to check the colours of my sunsets and gladioli but also would equip me with detailed wardrobes for my fictional characters. Critics would sneer at my prose and psychology but often praise the dress-sense of my women. I was cheating, but there is no art without cheating. That is why Plato and Tolstoy condemned literature.

I naturally now became shy of painting lessons and, in compensation, concentrated more on line, but drawing, especially vicious caricature, became more and more of a private activity. At the same time there began slowly to germinate what might be termed a synaesthetic faculty – a capacity to interpret the visual as the gustatory, and, much later, the auditory as the visual. I mean that I responded to a colour as if it were something to taste: this colour, which might not be that of a lemon, stung the tongue like a lemon; what might be black or deep purple nauseated like undercooked liver. When my father took me to a Hallé concert, I heard what I was told was an oboe as silver-green lemon juice; the flute was light brown and cold veal gravy. The urge to write for an orchestra, which came much later, was a compensation for painting the pictures I could not paint. Whatever the music critics say, I orchestrate well; I am in control of the tonal palette, or palate. When the tonal colours do not flash out, or when the mixture sounds wrong, it is always the fault of the conductor. I do not find a chromatic or tastebud analogy in words. I doubt if anyone does. The famous sonnet of Rimbaud, in which the vowels are given colour qualities, has everything to do with alchemy and nothing at all with visual perception.

Nineteen twenty-four was the year of the British Empire Exhibition at Wembley: I remember the commemorative postage stamp. What I most strongly remember is a newspaper photograph of the Prince of Wales sculpted in New Zealand butter. My imagination tasted the sailor prince. He smoked a pipe when he was not snapped smiling with a fag in his teeth, and the tobacco he smoked was called Baby's Bottom (smooth as a). We had this tobacco, its tin crawling with bare infants, on our shelves. My schoolmates doubted that such a proddy dog obscenity was possible. I brought five of them to the shop to prove that it was, but we happened to be out of stock at the time. This, like the colour blindness and the yearning for Joan Price, did me no good. I was a lone walker home – the tram depot, Bowes Road, Claremont Road (O claremont, O loving, O sweet Virgin Mary), Alison Street, Graeme Street, Great Western Street, Raby Street, 21 Princess Road, half a crown's worth of food on the tea table.

We had only one Christmas at 21 Princess Road. I was given fine presents – a conjurer's outfit, the *Chick's Own Annual* (my first book), a magic lantern with slides of jungle animals. I had been regularly patronizing the cinema next door, and there was a regular subsidiary feature called *Wild Life Round the World*. The Wilsons and the two Dwyer daughters, torpid after turkey, were to be shown a still but coloured version of this, and a candle was placed inside the magic lantern and lighted. '*Wild Life Round the World*,' I announced, and shoved in my first slide. Nothing appeared on the wall. The candle was too long. We had to wait till it burned down to lens-level, and Uncle Jimmy said: 'Play us something, Joe, while we're waiting.' So my father hammered out Musetta's song from *La Bohème*. Eventually the candle shortened, and the wild life roved stately on the wall that was a buff-coloured screen. What I cannot understand to this day is why the entire family agreed to wait on the candle's convenience. What was to stop our chopping it down to size? Were we stupid or merely torpid? I put this event or non-event into my early novel *Inside Mr Enderby*. Like T. S. Eliot's gamblers under the vine-crowned lintel or the white horse galloping in the meadow, this has remained as a symbol of something profound but unknowable. The image is accompanied by my stepmother's belching in the corner. She had become a great and loud belcher. 'Let it come up,' she told us. 'That's what the doctor says. You can always say excuse me.' But she never said excuse me.

How did I know it was Musetta's song my father played? He told me. It was the printed title above the music in one volume of many that had appeared in the sitting-room, the total compendium called *The Music Lover's Portfolio*. There was also *Music Masterpieces*, which came out in fortnightly parts. I do not know why there was this sudden incursion of middlebrow music – Boccherini's Minuet, a selection from *Madam Butterfly*, Tchaikovsky's Fifth Symphony in molecular instalments, also chatty articles by Tetrazzini, Percy Pitt and even Ernest Newman. I think that it was a matter of shopkeeper's reciprocity – a heavy-smoking music dealer had to be encouraged to fuel himself at Wilson's, 21 Princess Road.

My father did not now go at once to the Alexandra Hotel, or Big Alec, in contradistinction to the Little Alec on Alexandra Road, at five-thirty when it opened. He played the piano for a while out of *The Music Lover's Portfolio*. He did more. He played a march of his own composition which he had intended for the Royal Flying Corps. Then he complained of pains at the base of his spine which could be alleviated only by standing at a bar and drinking draught Bass. I was partly or wholly responsible for these pains. Working in the shop back room in shirtsleeves and bowler, he had stood to reach over for the daybook on the windoward side of the table. I had pulled his chair away and he sat down heavily on the floor. There was no malice in the act: it was something I had seen in comic papers and comic films. He may, after loud shouts to heaven all round, have interpreted it as a gesture of my desire for more notice than I was getting. He gave me this notice, though not much of it. I was seven now, and hence had arrived at the age of reason: I had to become a rational son of the Church by making my first confession and by taking my first communion. I needed advice about this confession, to be made in a dark box to Father O'Reilly at the Church of the English Martyrs. I had committed sins, I knew, and that removal of my father's chair had been one of them, but I was vaguely aware of a frontier between true peccancy and mere unacceptable social behaviour. For instance, nose-picking and deliberate farting could not be regarded by God the Father and Son (though I could see them going into earnest discussion about it) as acts worthy of hell. But there was a little song that I had been singing to myself, and I felt it was obscene enough to be sinful. What was the song, my father wanted to know. With shame I sang it:

There is a happy land far far away,
Where little piggies run three times a day.
Oh, you should see them run,
With their fingers up their bum,
Oh, you should see them run
Six times a day.

My father was grave about this, and said that I would have
to sing to an assembled congregation while the organ played
the tune. I did not, frankly, believe him. It struck me that,
in the manner of a proddy dog, he was poking fun at a holy
sacrament.

I did not have to sing the song. Father O'Reilly accepted
the generalized package of dirty words and bad thoughts,
and I received my absolution, though with, I thought, a
disproportionate penance of five Our Fathers and five Hail
Marys. The morning of my first communion should have
been the happiest moment of my life. It was, up to that
point, the most terrifying. I was given the body and blood
of Jesus Christ in the form of a thin wafer that cleaved to
the roof of my mouth, and I came away from the altar,
hands joined, eyes closed, murmuring 'My Lord and my
God.' I could clean Christ from my palate with my tongue,
but hellfire awaited if my teeth touched him. If even a morsel
of food or a droplet of liquid had preceded his ingestion,
then heaven would rage and fresh coal be trundled in against
my sudden and unrepentant death. It became, from the
48   moment of being a full communicant, very important to put

off death. I made my first communion with Manchester rain beating down. On my way to church I had opened my mouth to receive a few drops. Was that liquid nourishment? From now on, I had to be good. I had qualified for hell. My stepsister Madge was devout and over-scrupulous, far more so than the priests. Father Fitzjames at the Church of the Holy Name had thumped his evening paper (open at the racing page) and told her not to be a little fool. Father Myerscough had told her not to be disturbed at the incursion of some minuscule malice: the old boy, he said, had merely been tickling her with his tail. She was not convinced, and she passed on her fear of hell to me. It was all too easy to sin. Life, indeed, seemed all sin. I bought a twopenny sausage roll at Price's and then remembered it was Friday. I ate it nevertheless. Still chewing, I ran to evening confession. Swallowing the last flake, I began to whimper.

Both my stepsisters were courting, and presumably they permitted kisses but nothing else. The agony of the long courtship, as Graham Greene's whisky priest puts it, before the relief of marriage, the salty pretzels that exacerbate thirst for the cocktail. Agnes's marriage was to come first, and her fiancé was Jack Tollitt. *The Music Lover's Portfolio* was rightly of folio size, with great virgin flyleaves that cried out for ravishment with a pencil, and at the end of Volume One I drew Jack Tollitt. I emphasized his Nipponese buck teeth. He was a small, wiry, toothsucking Mancunian from Chorlton-on-Medlock, a follower of Manchester City football club, whose stadium at Maine Road was not far away from the shop, a Protestant undergoing slow instruction before being received into the Church, a condition of the impending marriage. He was now working in the shop, with the vigour and efficiency of one who foresaw a familial role in its running. My father was pleased to delegate responsibility. He had other interests than sitting bowler-hatted before cash books. He needed a longer lunchtime session in the Alec, where prolonged standing eased the pain at the base of his spine. In summer he liked to watch county cricket at Old Trafford; in winter he patronized the Manchester steeplechase meetings. Jack Tollitt had no time to shut me in a cardboard box, like Harold Smith. Harold Smith had left to emigrate to some corner of the Empire (the Wembley exhibition had, even at a Manchester remove, impressed him), and his successor had not lasted long: he had the habit of adding the date to the pounds, shillings and pence on the invoices. Jack and Agnes Tollitt were to set up their home at 21 Princess Road, which had three storeys and ample room for the breeding of a Catholic family. But residual Protestantism, as well as obstetric difficulties that were to oppress both my stepsisters, promoted an interest in Dr Marie Stopes's *Married Love*, and there was to be no philoprogenitiveness on the Irish pattern.

This proposed setting up of a new ménage at 21 Princess Road clinched the fulfilment of an enterprise that my step-mother had brooded on ever since the revelation that the new business was doing well. She was lonely without the noise, smoke and effluvia of drink and drama that had animated her life at the Golden Eagle. She wanted to be back, as she put it, in the public. A new pub was out of the question: it was unheard of to run one of those and a tobacco business as well. She compromised with a beer, wine and spirits store, an off-licence as it was termed, and there was one available at 261 Moss Lane East, a mere five minutes' walk from Princess Road. So she, who had so recently sold stock and goodwill in one place, now bought it in another. My father would not be concerned with the new venture. He would leave home for work in the morning like any other man, ready bowler-hatted, after his breakfast of a thick slice of pork pie and a pint of draught Bass, conveniently sleeping in its barrel on the premises. He would come home at three o'clock, when the Alec closed, for his lunch of grilled sweetbreads. He would fret in the house on Sundays over the *News of the World*, after the roast and the lemon pudding, his favourite, or only, dessert. The off-licence followed pub hours, and no evening family life was envisaged. Once more I was to see little of my father.

The off-licence was at the corner of Moss Lane East and Lincroft Street, where David Lloyd George had been born. A smaller and more radical politician lived on that street now, a man named Edwards, whose wife and children looked as if they had just served long stretches, for their heads were cropped to the limit. Their furniture was wooden boxes. 51

Edwards had ambitions to bring communism to the City Corporation, but he was never elected, since he could never put up the deposit. He would get up on a soap box on the rec, or recreation ground, a grim black gritty expanse at the head of Lincroft Street, and rant about the wrongs of the times, with a peroration on polluted Corporation water. Moss Side was a respectable district, and Edwards let down the tone. On the other hand he was all we had in the way of eccentricity and he had to be ambiguously cherished.

Our new shop, which was to end as a Caribbean shebeen, was very well patronized by Moss Siders who preferred to do their drinking at home. Their respectability was sometimes suspect: one old man came every evening with a jug for the supper ale and could be seen going home down an entry, where he would drink off a portion and make up the volume by urinating in the jug. When he was too old for this regular errand, his family complained about a loss of strength in the beer. Prim old ladies would come for a quarter bottle of gin, known in those cheap days as mother's ruin, and complain about the growing presence of black men in the town. These were probably Indians who had come to learn about cotton and ways of undercutting our major industry. 'They ought to be kept in their own country' was the usual judgement. An off-licence madam had to tolerate the prejudices of her customers, just like a pub landlady, and my stepmother had no difficulty there, for she subscribed to all the current bigotries. She would even, for the benefit of trade, agree with anticatholics who blamed the Pope for the coming war with America or alleged that the Eucharist was rank cannibalism. Haters of the Irish, who were many, met no opposition in her. Her Irishry was purely ancestral now, and she hid even that behind an English surname. England, she agreed with my father, was plagued by come-all-ye's and July barbers. A come-all-ye ('Come all ye good Irish and hark to my song / Of the butchers of England who did Ireland wrong') was an Irish immigrant rough, and a July barber was over to cut the harvest.

My stepmother did not improve as a character on the closer acquaintance now granted to me. She had few topics of talk beyond her days as a factory lass, an era of sweated freedom, when she and Katie 'Erbert got stuck in the works elevator or 'oist. This was not an anagram of Otis. She was rigorously consistent in her aitchlessness. When she said, as she regularly did, that she had a 'orrible 'eadache, she did not understand my father's wit when he said all she needed was a couple of aspirates. She picked her teeth with tram tickets and cleaned the wax out of her ears with hair-clips. Her teeth ached, just as her bunions did, and she had jealously stolen from my father his pains in the base of the spine. I would, perversely fascinated, tick off an anatomical manifest – head, nose, neck, chest, stomach, legs – and conclude that she was a symptomologist's gift. It seemed impossible to me that anyone so afflicted should wish to survive, but she maintained a large vigour. Occasionally she 53 would move out of the prison of pain, money and memory to speak of the world at large, which meant the royal family; the Old Queen, the Duke of Clarence who was really Jack the Ripper, King Teddy and the Jersey Lily (who dropped ice cream down King Teddy's back), Queen Mary's enamel maquillage. King Alphonsus and Queen Edna (sic, sic) of Spain once appeared on the margin. She recognized that foreign nations existed, since sherry had an Iberian provenance, and she had a respect for the Italians, of whom the Pope (dying from dropsy, she affirmed) was one. She was friendly with a Mrs Frascati, whose English was as aitchless as hers, and spoke once of seeing a woman in the street so beautiful and dark she had to be Italian. Gipsies frightened her, and she always bought their clothes pegs.

Her cooking remained good if plain, but she recognized no other arts. When we moved into 261 Moss Lane East, she gave Madge a handful of silver and told her to buy some second-hand pictures in the manner of buying oranges (no spotty or overripe ones allowed). So we had *The Light of the World* and *The Lady of Shalott* and *Dignity and Impudence* and even *The Stag at Bay*, as well as a few weeping moral anecdotes with bustles and Elgarian moustaches. In the bedrooms were pictures of the Pope blessing *urbem et orbem* and hagiographs straight from art-loving Dublin – the Sacred Heart, the Mater Dolorosa, St Anthony, St John the Baptist with an anachronistic infant Jesus. There were whatnots around, tenanted by a diminishing sequence of ebony elephants, a ringless ring tree, a ceramic girleen with her skirt wind-raised, a cloisonné dish bought in fear from a wandering Chinaman, a seashell ashtray (souvenir of Cleveleys), empty tortoiseshell spectacle cases, the remains of a doll's tea service, a backscratcher penitentially unemployed: we all wore wool next to the skin. There were no books even as part of the décor. Books were timewasters or worse. When, in my teens, I came home with a 1683 chapbook bought for twopence, she shrieked at it and put it on the fire with the tongs: she had heard of the Great Plague and here was a paper bubonic rodent.

People, even stepmothers, are not to be condemned for lack of art or aitches. I had no claim on her love and only a minimal one on what must be called her duty. She had accepted me as a pale thin adjunct of my father, whom draught Bass was rendering neither pale nor thin, and had to see me fed, clothed and educated up to the age of ten – or fourteen, when she had been apprised of the law. She herself had left school at ten, and this explained her illiteracy. Education did not guarantee success in the world, as witness my father, who had even been given piano lessons and yet spent his working time as an employee of M. Wilson, quondam Dwyer, née Byrne, and his leisure time boozing. Education for the priesthood was a different matter: you needed Latin for the Sunday hocus pocus. She saw from the start that I was not cut out to be a priest, and priests anyway were reserved to the Dwyer dynasty. She was to 55 frown later on my reading of books, but she was tolerant of *Comic Cuts* and *Funny Wonder* and *Film Fun*, which passed harmlessly through the system, did not have too many words, and could be used for lighting the kitchen fire. I had now graduated from the coloured nursery fodder of *Chick's Own* to the black and white vulgarity of Weary Willy and Tired Tim.

My Aunt Annie came sometimes to visit me, bringing on one occasion the gift of a half-crown gramophone which soon overwound. I should have conceived a nostalgia for the days when she seemed to be my first-hand mother, but, with a child's brutality, I rejected her as the president of damp, snakes, and a nightmare gipsy as well as, I now learned, an inadequate cuisine. She faded into her own greyness and died. Elsie and Betty, now called my cousins, occasionally wrote little letters. They were still writing them when I was a university student, and I objected to being addressed as Master Jack Wilson. But one of my fellow students said it sounded fine, like something Elizabethan. Elsie died single but Betty married after a long Lancashire courtship – twenty years, I believe. That was no record in Manchester. A lady named Miss Horrabin kept a newspaper and tobacco kiosk outside the Opera House on Quay Street, and she had been courted by a Mr Whittle for forty years. Of this couple the following was told, a typical Lancashire paring down to bare dialogue: 'Isn't it time we got wed, Jim?' – 'Ay, but who'd have us now?' I wrote to Betty congratulating her on her marriage and got a letter back telling me that, alas, her dear husband died on the wedding night. Excitement lethally exacerbated, said one of my pedantic friends, by excessive deferral. In Lancashire the comic and tragic easily mix.

PENGUIN 60s

ISABEL ALLENDE · *Voices in My Ear*

NICHOLSON BAKER · *Playing Trombone*

LINDSEY BAREHAM · *The Little Book of Big Soups*

KAREN BLIXEN · *From the Ngong Hills*

DIRK BOGARDE · *Coming of Age*

ANTHONY BURGESS · *Childhood*

ANGELA CARTER · *Lizzie Borden*

CARLOS CASTANEDA · *The Sorcerer's Ring of Power*

ELIZABETH DAVID · *Peperonata and Other Italian Dishes*

RICHARD DAWKINS · *The Pocket Watchmaker*

GERALD DURRELL · *The Pageant of Fireflies*

RICHARD ELLMANN · *The Trial of Oscar Wilde*

EPICURUS · *Letter on Happiness*

MARIANNE FAITHFULL · *Year One*

KEITH FLOYD · *Hot and Spicy Floyd*

ALEXANDER FRATER · *Where the Dawn Comes Up Like Thunder*

ESTHER FREUD · *Meeting Bilal*

JOHN KENNETH GALBRAITH · *The Culture of Contentment*

ROB GRANT AND DOUG NAYLOR · *Scenes from the Dwarf*

ROBERT GRAVES · *The Gods of Olympus*

JANE GRIGSON · *Puddings*

SOPHIE GRIGSON · *From Sophie's Table*

KATHARINE HEPBURN · *Little Me*

SUSAN HILL · *The Badness Within Him*

ALAN HOLLINGHURST · *Adventures Underground*

BARRY HUMPHRIES · *Less is More Please*

HOWARD JACOBSON · *Expulsion from Paradise*

P. D. JAMES · *The Girl Who Loved Graveyards*

STEPHEN KING · *Umney's Last Case*

LAO TZU · *Tao Te Ching*

DAVID LEAVITT · *Chips Is Here*